Life's Challenges

WEEKENDS WITH DAD

What to expect when your parents divorce

by Melissa Higgins

illustrated by Wednesday Kirwan

Saturday mornings were always super-loud at our house.
The morning Mum and Dad told us their big news, though,
it was quiet. That's how I knew something was wrong.

I thought my sister, Sam, and I were in trouble.

Mum and Dad sat us down in the living room. Mum said she and Dad had some problems. They had tried to work them out but couldn't. She said they loved Sam and me very much. But they weren't in love with each other anymore.

One out of four children in the UK lives with one parent.

"Mum and I will always be your mum and dad," Dad said. "But we're separating. We need some time apart."

Dad was moving to his own apartment.
Sam and I would live with Mum for now.

My heart pounded. I felt hot and cold at the same time. Why was Dad moving away?

Then I remembered. Last week Mum got cross when she saw the new football boots Dad had bought me. She and Dad had a huge fight over money. So it *was* my fault!

"You can return the shoes!" I shouted. "I don't need them!"

That's when Mum gave me a big hug. She said I hadn't done anything wrong. This was a grown-up problem.

Dad hugged me too.

Not too long after lunchtime, Dad left. I'd never felt so sad.

When parents are fighting a lot, some children feel relieved when their parents separate and the fighting stops. It's OK to feel relieved, scared, sad or angry. Everyone feels things differently.

On Monday morning, Mrs Niles went over our spelling words. All I could think about was Mum and Dad getting back together. Perry, my best friend, asked me what was wrong. I just shrugged. I couldn't tell him. I didn't want to talk to anybody.

Why hadn't Mum and Dad tried harder to fix their problems? Mums and dads can fix anything! Would Dad be OK by himself? Would Mum move away too? *Then* what would happen to Sam and me?

Why couldn't this happen to someone else?

Some children feel jealous of friends whose parents are still together. It may help to remember that even children with married parents don't have perfect lives.

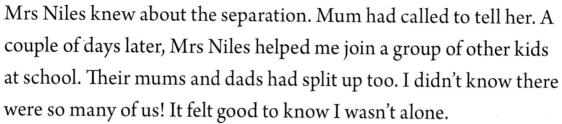

Mrs Niles knew about the separation. Mum had called to tell her. A couple of days later, Mrs Niles helped me join a group of other kids at school. Their mums and dads had split up too. I didn't know there were so many of us! It felt good to know I wasn't alone.

We get together every Wednesday. The other children understand how I'm feeling.

We usually sit on the floor in a big circle and talk about stuff. One thing I've learned: It's not good to keep feelings bottled up.

Our school counsellor, Miss Sanchez, is really nice. After we've finished talking, she lets us play games and hang out for a while.

11

I've learned a lot from the group. When I feel sad or angry, I kick my football.

When I don't understand something, I ask my mum or dad questions.

I call Dad when I miss him.

When I just need to talk,
I go to Mrs Niles or Perry.
They're both great listeners.

13

About a month after Dad moved out, Mum said she and Dad were going to get divorced. That meant they were splitting up for good. I sort of knew it was coming, but I still cried. Mum said she and Dad had to go to court. They had to work out child support and who would take care of my sister and me most of the time.

A woman from the court even talked to me. She asked a lot of questions, like where I wanted to live. I didn't want to hurt anyone's feelings. But she told me to be honest. I liked having a say.

It's strange living in two places. Sam and I share a room at Dad's but not at Mum's. We have a set of clothes and toys in both places. There's a big visitation calendar at both places too. The calendars remind us when we're supposed to be at which place.

On our first morning at Dad's, Sam said, "That's not how Mum makes pancakes."

I thought the same thing, but I shushed Sam anyway. I didn't want Dad to be upset.

The way things go at Dad's house may be different from the way things go at Mum's. It's OK to feel confused at first.

But Dad said it was OK. He wanted us to tell him when something bothered us. "I'll always love you two," he said. "No matter what." Then he asked us to help him make the pancakes.

Sam and I had fun helping. We made smiley faces with chocolate chips. Dad poured loops of blueberry syrup for hair. The pancakes were the best ever.

After a divorce, you may feel like you need to grow up quickly. But being a child is your only job.

It's been a year now since Mum and Dad got divorced. They both come to my games when they can. I still wish we lived together in one house. But I'm getting used to it.

What's not great is that when I'm with Dad, I miss Mum. When I'm with Mum, I miss Dad. Sometimes I feel like I'm living in two different worlds.

21

But Mum and Dad pay attention to me. And they're usually nice to each other. That really helps, because I love them both – a lot.

Just because we don't all live together anymore it doesn't mean Mum and Dad love me any less. Their love for me and Sam is forever.

Read more

Mum and Dad Glue, Kes Gray
(Hodder Children's Books, 2012)

*Standing on My Own Two Feet: A Child's
Affirmation of Love in the Midst of Divorce*,
Tamara Schmitz (Troubador Press, 2015)

Worried (Dealing with Feeling…),
Isabel Thomas (Raintree, 2014)

Website

**www.partnershipforchildren.org.uk/
resources/my-child-is-worried-about/divorce-
separation.html**

Divorce can be a big challenge for children. You can
grow through these family changes and discover
just how strong you really are.

Glossary

child support payments made to help with
children's living expenses

court place where legal decisions are made

divorce legal steps ending a marriage

separate choose to no longer live together

visitation time separated or time divorced
parents spend with their children

Index

Look out for all the books in the Life's Challenges series:

Goodbye, Jeepers

The Night Dad Went to Prison

Saying Goodbye to Uncle Joe

Weekends with Dad

Raintree is an imprint of Capstone Global Library Limited, a company incorporated in England and Wales having its registered office at 264 Banbury Road, Oxford, OX2 7DY – Registered company number: 6695582

www.raintree.co.uk
myorders@raintree.co.uk

Text © Capstone Global Library Limited 2016
The moral rights of the proprietor have been asserted.

Editor: Jill Kalz
Designer: Alison Thiele
Art Director: Nathan Gassman
Production Specialist: Sarah Bennett
The illustrations in this book were created with gouache and coloured pencil.

ISBN 978 1 4747 2468 5
20 19 18 17 16
10 9 8 7 6 5 4 3 2 1

British Library Cataloguing in Publication Data
A full catalogue record for this book is available from the British Library.

Acknowledgements
Thanks to our advisers for their expertise, research and advice:

Michele Goyette-Ewing, PhD Director of Psychology Training Yale Child Study Center

Terry Flaherty, PhD Professor of English Minnesota State University, Mankato

Every effort has been made to contact copyright holders of material reproduced in this book. Any omissions will be rectified in subsequent printings if notice is given to the publisher.

All the internet addresses (URLs) given in this book were valid at the time of going to press. However, due to the dynamic nature of the internet, some addresses may have changed, or sites may have changed or ceased to exist since publication. While the author and publisher regret any inconvenience this may cause readers, no responsibility for any such changes can be accepted by either the author or the publisher.

Made in China